GOD AND NOTHING ELSE

His Holiness Pope Shenouda III
117th Pope of Alexandria
Patriarch of the See of St. Mark the Evangelist

Published by

SAINT MARK COPTIC ORTHODOX
CHURCH OF CHICAGO
15 WEST 455 - 79TH STREET
BURR RIDGE, ILLINOIS 60521

September 12, 1991
Tout 1, 1708

H.H. Pope Shenouda III
117th Pope and Patriarch of Alexandria and
the See of St Mark

FOREWARD

In the name of the Father, the Son, and the Holy Spirit, one God, Amen.

Dear reader: This book is a collection of five lectures that were presented at St. Mark's Cathedral at Anba Rueiss Monastery. The lectures were as follows:

1. There is None upon Earth that I Desire Besides You ....Oct. 14, 1977
2. God is the Center of your Life ....Dec. 21, 1979
3. Being Satisfied with God .... Mar. 14, 1981
4. You ...and God ....Mar. 27, 1981
5. God...Your Only Goal ....Aug. 7, 1981

These lectures were consolidated to be offered in this book, which is one of a series of a larger book called, "God and Man." May God help us in publishing the rest of the book, through your prayers.

Pope Shenouda III

Contents

What is your Relationship with God?	1
The Lord is my Portion	15
There is None upon Earth that I Desire besides You	23
The Weak Points and the Substitutes	35
Gradual Progress	43

What is your Relationship with God?

Introduction

What is the importance of God in your life? Is there a relationship between you and Him? What is the nature of that relationship? What is its depth? Its extent? Is it a formal relationship? Or is there love and emotion in it? What is the importance of this relationship compared to other relationships?

The Importance of our Relationship with God

There are millions of people with whom you do not care to have a private relationship. However, God is the only Being with whom you should have a relationship. This relationship has special characteristics. This relationship is the only permanent relationship. You do not have a permanent relationship with every person you meet. You may separate from that person and you may have a different path in life, and it may be a superficial relationship. Your relationship with any person is limited to a specific area, which may end when it is finished. However, your relationship with God is not limited to your life on earth. It includes your eternity too. This relationship starts here and remains in eternity. Besides the fact that God created you and is taking care of you, He is the One who decides your fate in eternity. No doubt, this relationship is different from all other relations. Therefore, examine your relationship with God. Ask yourself these questions:

1. Do you know God? If you think you know Him, what is the nature of this knowledge and its depth?

2. Does God exist in your life? What kind of relationship do you have with Him?

3. Does God have priority in your love and your busy life?

4. Is God number one in your life? Is He everything to you? Is there something more important in your life besides God? What is it? Do you try to get rid of what competes with God in your heart?

There are different levels in the relationship with God. Where do you stand? Let us discuss these questions in details.

Do you know God? What is the depth of this knowledge? This may sound strange, for everyone thinks he knows God, but may only know that God exists. But we do not mean superficial mental knowledge, for even the devil knows that God exists. St. James said, "You believe that there is one God. You do well. Even the demons believe and tremble" (James 2:19). He means the dead unfruitful mental faith with no life in God.

Some existentialists believe that there is God in heaven and they make fun of that, saying, "Let God be in heaven and let Him leave the earth for us to enjoy." An example of this knowledge is a man who knows that electricity exists, but does not understand its nature, the way it works and has never used it.

Is your knowledge of God superficial? Do you know God only from books and sermons? Or is it an experience in your life and in your heart? Do you hear about God as you hear about distant nations that you have never visited? Is your knowledge about God limited to the walls of the church, and do you ignore Him once you are outside the church building? Is He the God existing only in seminaries and the dogmatic books?

The worst kind of knowledge is the knowledge without a relationship. You have to know God through experience and through living with Him. Henceforth, you know God who lives inside you and not the One you read about in books. Do you feel the tragedy which St.Augustine felt in his philosophy before he knew God when he said to Him, "You were with me, but because of my misery, I was not with you." God was with him, but he did not feel His presence.

Does God have a clear practical existence in your life?

Is God a mere idea or is He a true Being whom you feel and who has a practical existence in your life? Do you feel God's presence inside you? Who is God in relation to you? The question asked by Jesus to His disciples is still before us:

Who do you think I am? What kind of relationship do you have with God? Is it just a relationship of requests, on your side, and giving on God's side? Is God only the Giver who supplies all your needs, or is He the mere Helper who helps and gives you comfort? If He does not grant you His help, then, would you not have a relationship with Him? Or is He the One who solves your problems? If He does not solve them, then, would you not have a relationship with Him? Is God to you just a means, or is He your goal? Is He a means only to achieve your desires and to take things from Him? When you talk with Him, do you only demand of Him your requests, or do you give Him your heart, your love, and your time? Do you tell Him, "From Your hand, I have given You." If you want to demand things from God, do you want to take from Him His material gifts or His love and enjoyment? Truly, God goes around doing good.

But do you love God or only His blessings? God Himself or His gifts?

Do you rejoice when God gives you something and do not rejoice when you do not feel His gifts? If that is the case, this means that you rejoice with the gift and not the Giver. Hence, is your goal the gift and not God Himself? Do you love God only when He gives, but do not love Him when He does not give? I mean when you feel that He does not give, for God always gives whether you feel it or not.

If we believe that God always gives, we will feel unable to thank Him for all His gifts. We only know His apparent gifts, what about His hidden gifts? If God has ordered us to give in secret, He also gives in secret. His secret gifts are beyond our comprehension. Let us put aside the subject of giving, for our relationship with God should not be built on receiving gifts from Him.

Is your relationship with God a relationship of fear?

Do you walk with God and follow His commandments out of fear? Are you afraid of punishment and of the day of judgment when you stand in front of God giving an account of your life? Are you afraid because God is watching you and examining your thoughts and intentions and nothing is hidden from Him?

No one is afraid of the punishment of God except the guilty. Are you still in that stage and have not repented and reconciled with God? The Bible says, "The beginning of wisdom is the fear of the Lord." Are you still, then, in the beginning of the road and have not reached "Love which casts out fear" (1 John 4:18). as the apostle says?

Is your relationship with Him as that of a guilty to a Judge? He is the Master and you are a slave. He is a Judge who wants you to obey His rules and you are obliged to obey Him. He is the Mighty from whom you cannot escape and you have to follow His commandments whether you are convinced or not. If you are that type, then, you are still living in the bondage of the law and have not yet reached the life of grace, nor the life of purity whereby you love God's commandments and find them not hard. Then you may say with David, "The commandment of the Lord is pure, enlightening the eyes" (Psalms 19:8). "Oh, how I love Your Law" (Psalms 119:97). "How sweet are Your words unto my taste! Yea, sweeter than honey to my mouth" (Psalm 119:103). Have you reached the point at which you feel God's fatherhood to you, at least when you pray, "Our Father who are in heaven."

What is your relationship with God? Is it stil under trial?

Have you not reached the point of being confident in God and His love and promises? Are you still trying Him to see if He will answer you regarding this or that matter? Do you determine your relationship on that basis? You may either love Him or get angry with Him and stop going to His church or reading His Book, and start doubting what you have known about His qualities.

You know God is love. Do you believe that all that God plans for you is full of love, even if it does not appear to be like that? What is your relationship with this love? Are you filled with love towards God and His people? Do you feel that God is working with you? God also is truth. What is your relationship with the truth? If you are away from the truth, then you are away from God.

Does your relationship with God have love, fellowship and life in Him? Can you tell Him, "I am for My Beloved and My Beloved is for me." (Song of Solomon 6:3) I know that you believe in God as the Creator, the Master, the Shepherd, and the Judge. But do you consider Him also as a Lover of Mankind and especially a Lover of yourself?

Is God number one in your life? Do you tell God in your prayers, "When I knew You and tasted Your love, all other kinds of love and emotions became so insignificant. Your love is the only deep love."

Does your love to God make you love to talk to Him? Are your prayers full of love and emotions toward God; and likewise are all the other spiritual means? Blessed are you if you are this type of person. However, if you are not, you had better wake up lest you should hear this voice rebuking you, "These people draw near to Me with their mouths and honor Me with their lips, but have removed their hearts far from Me" (Isaiah 29:13).

God does not require anything from your relationship with Him except love. He does not request anything from you except your heart. "My son, give me your heart." When Jesus saw Peter after the resurrection, He did not tell him, "Why did you deny Me, or how did you become so weak or what did you mean when you insulted Me and said, 'I do not know the Man'?" He asked him only one question, "Do you love Me?" (John 21:15). When Peter replied , "You know everything, you know that I love You." Then the Lord told him, "Feed My sheep." He does not require anything except love.

Many exercises or one exercise? Someone asked this question, "When I read the Bible, I discover a new virtue for which I want to train myself. The more I read, the more I discover another virtue and so on. So how can I train myself for all these various virtues? Where do I start? Which one do I postpone? Because the exercises are so many, I forget most of them." However, God's love includes all virtues. If you train yourself in God's love, then you will find yourself trained in all other virtues. It is the only complete exercise which if you master, you will not need other exercises. But God's love has to be a pure, deep love with understanding, in which you prefer God to any other desire. Any one might say, "I love God." However, he should be asked, "Does God have priority in your heart? Does God's love satisfy your heart, so that you do not need any other love?" If you have true love to God, certainly you will feel satisfied.

True love to God liberates the heart from any other kind of love.

Our love to God is very deep so that all other kinds of love become superficial. God's love rules the whole heart, and all other kinds of love which do not proceed from God's love are cast away so God becomes everything to us. God's love liberates man from any other desire against God. If a person is enslaved by any desire, then this desire pulls him down and dominates him. Therefore, he loses part of his true inner freedom.

How can one be freed from all other desires? One is freed when a stronger and deeper love replaces all other kinds of love and casts them away. There is nothing stronger than God's true love because it liberates man from all his desires. One sees that anything outside God is not an enjoyment, and God becomes the desire of the soul. One of the saints said, "Repentance is replacing one kind of love by another, replacing the love of the world, the flesh, and materialism by God's love." Has God's love reached that level in your heart? Has it liberated you from all other desires?

Even in eternity, the eternal joy is God. There is no eternal joy besides God, and any other joy besides God is not a true joy. The perfect eternal joy with God is what no eye has seen nor ear heard. This is the true kingdom, to live with God and in God forever without any obstacles.

God's love liberates man from all desires and fears. We mean that no other desire enslaves man. As Saint Paul said, "All things are lawful for me, but all things are not helpful. All things are lawful for me, but I will not be brought under the power of any." (1 Corinthians 6:12) The example of the bird is very illustrative. The bird finds a place that has many grains, so it picks one or more, then flies away without getting attracted to that place or to these grains, and without storing any of them.

Whoever loves God is not afraid of anything. A person is fearful if he has a desire for something which he cannot obtain, or if he has that thing but is afraid of losing it. If God's love has liberated you, then whom are you afraid of? Nothing. But you may say with St. Augustin, "I sat on top on the world when I felt that I do not desire nor fear anything." Then your heart will be filled with strength, and you may say with Saint Paul, "Who shall separate us from the love of Christ? Shall tribulation or distress or persecution, or famine or nakedness or peril or sword? In all these things, we are more than conquerors through Him who loved us." (Romans 8: 35-37)

God's children are free in their inner life. God's love has liberated them and granted them purity, self-deprivation, power and courage. It removed all other desires and made them free as the light of the sun or the fresh air.

Has anyone asked you: "What is God in relationship to you?" Hopefully you say, "He is the Beloved whose left hand is under my head and Whose right hand embraces me." (Song of Solomon 2: 6) "I cannot live without His fellowship, because through Him, I exist, live and move. He is not a mere idea, but He is existing in my spirit, my blood, and my thought. He is everything to me." "O Lord, You work in me, You guide me and lead me. You work with me and inside me. I may not comprehend You, but I feel You inside me with a spiritual comprehension. I know You, but words are too weak to explain this knowledge."

You are not outside me, but inside me. When I remember You, I do not only lift up my eyes to heaven because You are not only up in heaven, but inside me. I do not seek You outside . It is true what the poet said, "I closed up my eyes so I can see You." You are above the senses. I get rid of my senses so I can find You. However, if my mind is occupied with the senses: sight, hearing, touch, then they will hinder me from seeing You. "I wish I could forget everything and You alone stay with me to satisfy my life."

The problem of our Father Adam was the additions that entered his heart and mind besides God. In the beginning, God was everything to Adam's life. But when he sinned, many things entered his life. Satan offered him knowledge to love it instead of God. He offered him the love of godship and tempted him that he and Eve will become gods like God. (Genesis 3:5) He offered him a tree and a fruit to eat. He showed him that the fruit was appealing to the eye and good to eat; therefore, the enjoyment of the senses and the lust of the flesh entered his life. In conclusion, the devil offered him new things to invade his heart and become more important to

How can I win? When? How can I excel and establish myself, my position, my reputation, my finance, my pleasure, my freedom, my honor, etc....

The self takes the first place and not God. While you are thinking of yourself, you may forget God. You may not give God any time or attention. You may even break God's commandments to build yourself up or please it the way you like.

What was the problem of the existentialists except themselves. The existentialist wants to feel his existence and enjoy that existence by indulging in the pleasures of this world and by having complete freedom with no obstacle or law or tradition or divine commandment to hinder it! He may see that God is limiting that freedom, therefore, he may reject God for the enjoyment of himself. "He that finds his life, shall lose it." (Matthew 10:39) The motto of the existentialist is one of the worst examples. They may resemble the Epicurians whose goal is enjoyment, and whose motto is, "Let us eat and drink, for tomorrow we shall die." They mean, "Let us enjoy ourselves before we die." Likewise, do all those who walk according to the desires of the flesh.

There are other examples for the dominion of the self: King Herod is one of them. King Herod did not rejoice when Jesus was born, but thought of himself. How can there be another king for the Jews besides him? Therefore, he ordered the killing of all the children under two. He did not rejoice like the wise men or the shepherds, whose self did not hinder them from God!

King Herod who killed James the apostle, and who imprisoned Peter, when he sat on his throne arrayed in royal apparel and made an oration unto the people, they kept shouting saying, "The voice of a god and not of a man." Immediately, the angel of the Lord smote him because he did not give God the glory and he was eaten by worms and died. (Acts 12: 21–23)

Pilate also cared for himself and not for the Lord Jesus. In spite of his saying, "I find no fault in Him," he betrayed the Lord Jesus because he was afraid to lose his position and wanted to please Caesar. Moreover, he wanted to justify himself, so he washed his hands saying, "I am innocent of the blood of that Righteous."

The self was able to destroy kings, chief priests and governors

him than God. He sacrificed God for them. God did not become everything to Adam, but he found in his heart what competed with Him! God became a part of a group! God no longer ruled over all the love inside the heart, but many other kinds of love, penetrated the heart like the love of knowledge, the love of becoming gods, the love of food, the lust of the senses. In summary, the self competed with God in importance. As days and generations pass, many other kinds of love have penetrated the heart at the expense of God's prime importance in the heart. The more one loves these matters, the less is his love to God. What is the solution then? No doubt, it is forsaking all these matters.

Are you ready to forsake things for God's sake? The rich ruler could not forsake his money; therefore, he left the Lord feeling very disappointed. Adam and Eve could not forsake the temptaion of knowledge and being divine; therefore, they lost their divine image. Can we learn a lesson in forsaking?

If we cannot forsake everything for the Lord, can we give the tithes and the first-born to the Lord? Can we forsake being busy one day a week to devote it to God? Can you forsake some of the enjoyment which fills your heart so your heart may be clear for God? Can you forsake some kinds of food so your spirit may grow during fasting. You have to be ready to forsake something for God's sake.

If God has priority in your heart, then you can forsake things for Him. You can forsake everything for God because everything will be a trifle and lose its value besides God. You will know that one day you have to leave everything for Him, and even leave the whole world. Therefore, it is better for you to leave the world willingly than leave it unwillingly. This is what St. Anthony learned when he saw his father's dead body. When you forsake something for God, you prove that your love to God has exceeded that thing. If you forsake everything for God, you prove that your love to God is more than your love to anything else.

The most important thing to forsake for God is yourself. Many people concentrate on themselves. Their ego is the center of their thoughts. All that they care for is themselves What is my condition now? What do I desire to be? How to be it? When? What are the obstacles in front of me?

and make them perish. They betrayed Jesus because of envy, for they were afraid to lose their positions. The Pharisees said to one another, "You see that you are accomplishing nothing. Look the world has gone after Him." (John 12:19) Because of jealousy, they drifted away from God. They paid money to Judas to betray His Master. They brought false witnesses, and they bribed the soldiers to say that His disciples came at night to steal the body while they were sleeping! All that because they loved themselves, their positions and fame! But they never thought of the kingdom of God. Also, they did not care for the prophecies of salvation and redemption. Moreover, they ignored teaching the people and leading them to the faith. All that concerned them was how they could exalt their self-image in front of the people, even if they had to destroy the Messiah.

John the Baptist rebuked all those Pharisees because he did not care for his ego. He got rid of every attention given to him and he directed it to Jesus saying, "He who is coming after Me is mightier than I, whose sandals I am not worthy to carry." (Matthew 3:11) He also said, "He who has the bride is the bridegroom, but the friend of the bridegroom, who stands and hears him, rejoices greatly because of the bridegroom's voice. Therefore, this joy of mine is fulfilled. He must increase, but I must decrease." (John 3: 29,30) Magnificent glory surrounded John the Baptist, but he did not let this glory enter his heart. His self did not occupy his life, but God only occupied it. He came to prepare the way for the Lord, therefore, he denied himself and said about the Lord, "He who comes from above is above all." (John 3: 31)

Love of self leads to envy and envy destroys love. Love does not envy. When one envies, he concentrates on himself and he loses the love toward the one he envies. If he loses love, he loses God, for God is love. Joseph's brothers sold him and deceived their father. They did not set God's love first, because they loved themselves and did not accept that Joseph would be better than them. Beware that envy or anger remove the love from your heart lest you should lose God who does not dwell in a heart free from love. "If you cannot love your brother whom you see, how can you love God whom you do not see?" (1 John 4: 20)

When the self is proud, it rejects God. A good example for

this is the fall of Satan He said in his heart, "I will ascend into heaven, I will exalt my throne above the stars of God; I will also sit on the mount of the congregation on the farthest side of the north; I will ascend above the heights of the clouds, I will be like the Most High." (Isaiah 14: 13,14) The result was that he fell into Hades. His self pride made him compete even with God.

The builders of the tower of Babel wanted to be better than all those living on earth. They said, "Come, let us build ourselves a city, and a tower whose top is in heaven; let us make a name for ourselves, lest we be scattered abroad over the face of the whole earth." (Genesis 11: 4) The result was that God made them speak different languages and scattered them. Therefor, whoever exalts himself is abased and loses God. However, he who puts himself in front of God's unlimited greatness, sees that he is only dust and ashes, and therefore, he feels humble and broken hearted.

The war against the ego has raged the saints also. The twelve apostles were also tempted and thought who would sit at the right hand of Jesus and who would be the first. Jesus, who knew that the ego will deviate man from God, told the disciples, "Let not this thought be in you. Whoever wants to be first, let him be last and a servant to all." He gave them an example when He washed their feet. Also, when they rejoiced that the devils submitted to them, Jesus told them, "Do not rejoice for that." Real joy is not the ego, but in cleaving to the Lord and His love, hence our names will be written in the Book of Life.

The ego has tempted a great prophet like Jonah. He was concerned about his ego and his word. When God told him to instruct the people of Ninevah that God would destroy their city, he fled from Him, knowing that He is merciful. When the whale spat him out and he preached in Ninevah and the people repented, he did not rejoice at the great salvation that God had made, because he concentrated on his dignity and his word. He sat very sad; then God told him, "Is it right for you to be angry?" (Jonah 4: 4) Jonah answered, "It is right for me to be angry, even to death!" (Jonah 4: 9) Thus, Jonah's will was opposed to God's will and his feelings were the opposite of God's. All that was because he concentrated on his ego. If it weren't for God who looked for him and taught him a lesson, he would have perished.

Also, Job, the righteous, was tempted by his ego. He was a righteous man, but his problem was that he knew that he was righteous. He said, "I am blameless, yet I do not know myself. Though I were righteous, my own mouth would condemn me; though I were blameless, it would prove me perverse." (Job 9:20,21). Therefore, it was mentioned that Job was righteous in his own eyes (Job 32:1). He pleaded with God saying, "Do not condemn me, show me why You contend with me. Does it seem good to You that You should oppress the work of Your hands, and shine on the counsel of the wicked?" (Job 10:2,3) But he was severe with his friends.

Job was tempted till he was freed from his self pride and was humbled and said, "Behold I am vile; what shall I answer You? I lay my hand over my mouth." (Job 40:4) "I have uttered what I did not understand, things too wonderful for me, which I did not know...You said, "I will question you and you shall answer Me."......Therefore I abhor myself, and repent in dust and ashes (Job 42:3–6). When Job reached the dust and ashes, "The Lord then raised his face and restored his captivity" (Job 32:29,10).

Man has to be free from his self, or God has to liberate him from it. God freed Job from his pride, money, riches health, and the respect of men. He has freed him from his ego and from his dependance on his understanding and wisdom. Finally, Job put his hand on his mouth and repented in dust and ashes saying, "I am vile, what shall I answer You?" (Job 40:4) Then God removed the temptation.

Do you know to what extent the danger of the self is? When one is over-confident in himself, in his thinking, capabilities, intelligence, then he will brag about himself and not demand the advice of others. The Bible says, "There is a way which seems right to a man, but its end is the way of death" (Proverbs 14:12).

When our Father Jacob cared for his ego, he fell into many troubles. To receive his father's first-born blessing, he had to use non Christian ways like lying and deceiving. Then he was exposed to his brother's anger, became very frightened and had to escape.

When the ego wants to fulfill its desires, it may use unlawful methods so it loses its spirituality, and often the satisfaction of the ego becomes the goal.

God becomes only a means to fulfill the ego and its goals. God does not become the goal, which one sacrifices for. Even all prayers become concentrated on requests to build the ego, even if it contradicts God's will. In this case, prayers of praise which contain the element of love and meditation disappear.

The lord Jesus has given us an example in emptying Himself. In His incarnation, we read, "He emptied Himself." To what extent? To the extent that He became a slave. He obeyed till death, death on the cross (Philippians 2:7-9).

On the cross, He presented Himself a sacrifice to please God the Father and to fulfill the Divine Justice. He presented Himself a sacrifice of sin to save humanity, whose sins He carried. "He was numbered with the transgressors" (Isaiah 53:12).

He said to the Father, "Not my will, but your will," presenting Hismelf on the altar of obedience.

St. Paul learned to empty Himself when he said, "Not I live, but Christ lives in me" (Galatians 2:20).

Who can say with St. Paul, "Not I live?" Let us examine ourselves and let God become everything to us, all our emotions, all our heart, love and hope. We prefer Him to everything else and we find all our enjoyment and pleasure in Him, so we may sing with Jeremiah the prophet saying "The Lord is my portion, says my soul, therefore, I hope in Him" (Lamentations 3:24).

The Lord is my Portion

The Lord is my Portion, says my soul. Lamentations 3:24

We all repeat this beautiful phrase and we memorize it, but who can live it and implement it in his life? Who takes it as a spiritual principle that spares him many commandments? Do you accept that the Lord becomes your portion in this life?

Many may consider home, wife, children, position, money, job, authority, and fame as their portion; and they do not mind to add God to all these! However, to have God as our sole portion (Psalms 16:5), and to be satisfied with God and to feel that we do not need anything besides Him (Psalms 23:1), is not easy for everyone to live it. However, God gave us such good examples from the Holy Bible.

He gave us an example in the priests of the Old Testament. The example was not only the priests but the Levite Tribe who devoted their lives to the service of the Lord. "Therefore, Levi has no portion nor inheritance with his brethren; the Lord is his inheritance, just as the Lord your God promised him" (Deuteronomy 10:9). Hence, their names became "Ekleros", that is portion, for the Lord was their portion and they also were a portion to the Lord. The Lord used to satisfy them, therefore, they did not need a thing. Their lives became a portion to the Lord. No land nor property nor any other work used to occupy them except the Lord.

Are you the same? Is the Lord your portion? If you are not one of the devoted people, examine your relationship with God at least in the light of these examples:

If your life is not a portion to the Lord, is Sunday the Lord's portion? If you do not give all your life to God, do you give Him at least the Lord's

Day? Do you consecrate the Lord's Day, that is, do you not do any of your daily routine work according to God's commandment? (Deuteronomy 5:14) Do you devote it to prayer, meditation, spiritual reading, God's service and His enjoyment? Or are you busy with other things?

If you cannot give one day to the Lord, then this means that the Lord is not your portion. If He were your portion, you could have controlled your many cares and busy life and found the time for Him, and the Lord's Day would have been set for Him.

Another test for showing that the Lord is your portion is prayer. If you are not regular in your prayers, then this means that the Lord is not your portion and that He does not satisfy you nor fill your heart! When you stand to pray, many thoughts come to your mind and you think when your prayers will be finished, so you may have the time to accomplish your little jobs which, unfortunaltely, you consider more important than prayer! If these thoughts were mere temptations from the devil, then you would have been annoyed and you would have continued praying and found enjoyment in so doing. However, if you want to finish your prayer fast because of the other cares of life, then this is a proof that God is not your poriton.

Whoever chooses the Lord to be his portion, if he stands to pray, he does not like to stop praying, and forgets about all other concerns. If he remembers them, they seem to be trifles which do not deserve to keep his heart or mind busy.

Whoever chooses the Lord to be his portion, finds joy and enjoyment in the Lord. He rejoices in the Lord and enjoys sitting at His feet and talking to Him. He says with David the Psalmist, "I will lift up my hands in Your Name. My soul shall be satisfied as with marrow and fatness" (Psalm 63:4,5).

When a person rejoices in the Lord, he devotes more time to God and makes God enter deep to his heart, his love, his attention and concern.

Some people may find joy in carnal matters. This proves that they have not taken the Lord to be their portion. If this is the case, let me ask: What is your relationship with God? Do you have any relationship with Him at all? Does He exist in your life? Is He on the margin of your life? Is He the center of your life? Is He all your life? Is He one of your hopes in life? Or is He all your hope? Is He part of your concerns? Or is He all that concerns you?

Is God a theory that you read about in the books? Or is He a mere teaching that you learned about in the church? Or is He a practical existence in your life? Be frank with yourself and do not deceive yourself. I say that because some may pray, fast or have communion, but God is still at the corner of their lives and not in the depth! When will God be the whole life? When will we say with St Paul, "For me to live is Christ" (Philippians 1:21)?

The main concern for some is their family, position, money, marriage, children, entertainment. If one does not have these things, people might say, "That person is not enjoying life."

He who says, "For me to live is Christ" can continue to say, "And to die is gain." He can also say, "I am hard pressed between the two, having a desire to depart and be with Christ, which is far better" (Philippians 1:23). Moreover, he can say, "Who shall separate us from the love of Christ? Shall trouble, tribulation, or persecution, or hunger or nakedness or danger or sword? As it is written for your sake we are killed all day long, we are accounted as sheep for the slaughter. Yet in all these things, we are more than conquerors through Him who loved us" (Romans 8:35–37).

Another test of your relationship with God is this commandment, "You shall love the Lord your God with all your heart" (Deuteronomy 6:5). You may love God with your heart, but do you love Him with all your heart? Do you give Him all your heart and all your love? Who is able to apply this commandment?

Who has all his emotions and feelings concentrated on God? God is his poriton here on earth and there in eternity. God fills his life, his mind, and his heart.

When God rules all of a person's heart, then the whole world becomes to him like a garbage can with no value at all. He looks at all the pleasures of life and says, "Vanity of vanities, all is vanity. All is vanity and grasping for the wind" (Eccelesiastes 1:2, 14). Money, position, popularity, beauty, glory, house, and children, all are vain and God becomes everything to that person and everything besides Him is worthless.

Sit quietly by yourself and examine your relationship with God. Where is its position on the map of God?

What is the position of God in your life and feelings? Tell yourself: Does God satisfy me entirely to the extent that I do not need anything besides Him and I do not feel that I miss anything? Am I happy that I have found God? Do I sing to Him a new song every day? Is the name of the Lord beloved and on my lips?

Is the Lord my dream at night and my hope in the day time? Are all my emotions in Him? Is He my life? What is His position in my life? Now and then, you need to examine yourself and your goals. Is God your goal in life? Is He your portion? Is He your goal all the time or occasionally? Do you have other goals that replace God in your heart and become your portion in life?

Look at David, what was God's place in David's life? David says, "My strength and praise is the Lord" (Psalms 118). Also, he says, "Our Lord is our Refuge, Strength, and Help in all our tribulations" (Psalms 45). He goes on and says that the Lord is His shield. Moreover, he tastes God and sees how kind He is. God is everything to him.

All those who took the Lord to be their portion, found that He is everything to them.

They do not fight for themselves, for the Bible tells them, "The Lord will fight for you, and you shall hold your peace" (Exodus 14:4).

They do not talk for themselves, but "The Spirit of their Father talks in them" (Matthew 10:20). "He gives them word and wisdom that no one can oppose" (Luke 21:15). He is "The One who guides them in victory" (2 Corinthians 2:14). "He overshadows them with His wings." He is the Father, the Beloved, the Friend and Companion on the road.

He is the Only heart guaranteed in His love and sincerity. We may not guarantee the emotions and feelings of people or their sincerity in all circumstances. They may leave their first love. However, God is the Only One guarnateed in His love. Even if we ae not faithful to Him, He remains faithful. (Timothy 2:13) If a mother forgets her baby, He never foegets us, for He has inscribed us on the palms of His hands. Even the hairs of our head are all numbered and none falls without His permission. How can we not love such a God?

Is God the source of all goodness or is He Goodness Himself? A beginner in the spiritual life and in his relationship with God may look to God as the source of all goodness. Definitely, this is true, but whoever takes God as his portion, sees that God is Good Himself and the only Goodness. He does not look for pleasure away from God or as a reward from Him, but sees that God is the true pleasure that he enjoys.

God is everything in eternity. Eternity is not pleasure except with God. He is the Tree of Life upon whom we nourish. He is the Hidden Manna, the Bread of Life, the Water of Life who quenches the thirst of everyone who drinks from Him. He is the Life, whoever abides in Him abides in life. He is the Truth, whoever knows Him, knows the truth and the truth liberates him. He is the True Light who enlightens every person. He is the Wisdom and the True Pleasure.

God will not grant us a specific thing to please us in eternity, but He Himself is our pleasure. Whoever comes closer to Him, comes closer to the real happiness. Whoever tastes Him, tastes happiness and love. Are we going to be busy in eternity or have pleasure in anything besides God? Definitely no. God, who is our portion here, will be our portion there in eternity.

How can our permanent enjoyment be in Him? This is the secret of the Kingdom. This is what no heart has ever thought of. For all that we enjoy here on earth in our relationship with God is not comparable with the glory which will be revealed in us when we know Him the true knowledge and grow in His knowledge all the time. Our Lord Jesus said to the Father, "This is eternal life that they may know You" (John 17:3).

If God fills all your heart and thoughts, and if He is all your love and goal, then how can you sin? It is impossible, for sin is deviation from God's love to another kind of love against Him. However, if God is your portion, goal, hope, and the desire of your heart, then you cannot sin and the devil cannot touch you. This is how God's children are manifest. (1 John 3:9,10)

Your love to God does not give any chance for sin. Then you do not need many exercises to train yourself in many conmmandments, but His love suffices you and that is your only exercise.

The difference between Law and Grace appears here. Whoever is still under the law, struggles with all his might to obey the commandment. However, if one is within the Divine love and God becomes his portion, then love liberates him from the dominion of the Law. Through His love to God, he does all good, loves virtue and the commandment, and God's commandments are not felt as a burden on him and do not require any effort from him.

Grace does not destroy the commandment or the Law, for keeping the commandments becomes an expression for God's love. It is no more orders, to do this and not to do that. The Lord said, "If you love Me, keep My commandments" (John 14:15). Hence, keeping God's commandments comes naturally as a result of our love to God.

If God is your portion, then you will not falter between two opinions. You will not be with the Lord one day and another day away from Him. The heart, which is steadfast in God's love, will not deviate nor change from his Divine goal. Hence, the Lord says, "Abide in my love" (John 15:9). "Abide in Me and I in you as the branch abides in the Vine" (John 15).

Are you like the branch abiding in the Vine? The juice of the vine goes in its veins and grants it life. Through this abiding, the branch resembles the vine in everything and gives fruit of the vine itself. The vine becomes the portion of the branch. If the branch separates from the vine, it separates completely from life. It dries up, dies, and is thrown in fire. However, while abiding in the vine, it survives and grows too. Hence, the Lord said, "I am the Vine, you are the branches" (John 15:5).

Hence, if the Lord is your poriton, He will be inside you, like the juice of the vine which is inside the branch. Saint Paul said, "Do you not know that you are the temple of God and the Spirit of God dwells in You?" (1 Corinthians 3:6) Since God is inside you, why do you seek Him outside you? "If anyone says to you, Look here is the Christ! or there' do not believe it." (Matthew 24:23) He is inside you. "I in them" (John 17:23).

If the Lord is your portion, do you feel His presence inside you? Are you "Theophorus" which means the carrier of God? Saint Agnatius from Antioch was thus called. Every true believer in whose heart the Lord dwells and who feels His presence wherever he goes, is a carrier of God.

I hope you pray saying, "Lord, be my only portion, and I do not want any other portion besides you. Take everything I have and give me Yourself.

Give me the privilege of your knowledge. I do not want to request many things, for I only want You. I want everything to be worthless, and you become the only worthwhile Being whom I care for, so I may love You, who are living in my heart, and not only know You from books."

Examples of Saints who have taken the Lord as their Portion

1. Saint Peter: He said, "We have left all and followed You" (Matthew 19:27). He expressed the condition of all the apostles who have forsaken their families, jobs, and followed the Lord who became their portion.

2. Saint Paul: Became one of the apostles. Listen to his beautiful expression, "I have suffered the loss of all things, and count them as rubbish, that I may gain Christ" (Philippians 3:8). In Saint Paul's eyes, everything became worthless. Therefore, he said, "What things were gain to me, these I have counted loss for Christ. But indeed I also count all things loss for the excellence of the knowledge of Christ Jesus my Lord" (Philippians 3:7,8).

3. The Psalm says to every soul who becomes a bride to the Lord, "Listen O daughter, consider and incline your ear, forget your own people also and your father's house; so the king will greatly desire your beauty, because He is your Lord, worship Him" (Psalm 45:10,11).

4. Our Mother Rebecca, who left her country and family and went with Eleazor, the servant, to marry Isaac, became a symbol of the human soul who forsakes everything to live with Christ as her Portion.

Here we remember a beautiful expression said by David the prophet, "There is none upon earth that I desire besides You" (Psalm 73:25).

There is None upon Earth that I Desire besides You

There is none upon earth that I desire besides You .   Psalms 73:25

Whoever loves God deeply reaches the point where he or she is satisfied with God. God fills his heart, thoughts and feelings and satisfies him; hence he says with David, "I shall not want" (Psalm 23). He feels that he cannot add anything to God in his heart; therefore, he lives happily with God and says in love, "There is none upon earth that I desire besides You." Our fathers the saints followed that example and God filled their lives with His presence.

David the Prophet

David the prophet as an example. He was a king, with all the authority and greatness of the kingdom. He was a leader of the army, judge of the people, head of a big family, respected by everyone. He did not lack any of all the pleasures of the world. However, all that did not fill his heart, but he said, "One thing I ask of the lord." What is that one thing that you lack , O great king? He says, "One thing I have desired of the Lord that I may dwell in the house of the Lord all the days of my life" (Psalm 27:4). In this holy place, he sought God saying, "Your face Lord I will seek. Do not hide Your holy place from me" (Psalm 27:8,9).

Is this your only request? What about the kingdom, the army, the court, the family, your riches? No, Lord, "There is none upon earth that I desire besides You." "O God, you are my God, early will I seek You. My soul thirsts for You, my flesh longs for You" (Psalms 63:1). "My soul follows close behind You" (Psalms 63:8). "I will lift up my hands in Your name. My soul shall be satisfied as with marrow and fatness." "Your lovingkindness is better than life, my lips shall praise You" (Psalms 63:3). When I remember You on my bed, I meditate on You in the night watches" (Psalms 63:6).

This is the love which fills the heart. David says, "Oh, how I love Your Law! It is my meditation all the day."

What about your cares, David?

All my cares do not keep me busy. "Seven times I praise You, because of Your righteous judgment" (Psalm 119:164). "At midnight, I will rise to give thanks to You" (Psalm 119:62). "My eyes are awake through the night watches, that I may meditate on Your word" (Psalm 119:48). "How sweet are your words to my taste, sweeter than honey to my mouth" (Psalm 119:103).

<u>Truly whoever loves God, considers everything as a trifle in his eyes.</u> David was not tempted by his palace or his throne, but he said, "How amiable are Your tabernacles, O Lord of hosts, my soul longs, yea even faints for the courts of the Lord" (Psalm 84:1). "I was glad when they said to me, 'let us go into the house of the Lord'" (Psalm 122:1). "I would rather be a doorkeeper in the house of my God" (Psalm 84:10). Why? "For a day in Your courts is better than a thousand" (Psalm 84:10). "I have desired none of the earth besides You." This expression is a true expression of the fervent heart and of one's relationship with the Lord.

Abraham

Another example is our Father Abraham. When God called Abraham, He told him, "Get out of your country, from your kindred and from your father's house, to a land that I will show you" (Genesis 12:1). Abraham left his country, his family, and his father's house, and said to the Lord, "I have desired none from the earth besides You." He followed the Lord without knowing where he was going (Hebrews 11:8). It was sufficient that he was following the Lord. He did not care about the place he was going to, where it was or what it was like. But all his thoughts were in the Lord who accompanied him.

When Tarah his father accompanied him, he was delayed some time in Haran (Genesis 11:31). When Lot, his nephew, accompanied him, a fight broke out between Lot's shepherds and Abraham's shepherds. When Lot was separated from him and chose the most fertile land in the region, God's blessings were multiplied in Abraham's life.

How are you going to live, Abraham, and Lot has chosen all the plain of Jordan and has left poverty for You? (Genesis 13:11). Abraham says, "I am with God, and I do not desire anything from the world. The Lord and His grace are sufficient for me." The Lord blessed him and told him, "Lift your eyes and look from the place where you are, northward, southward, eastward, and westward; for all the land which you see I give to you and your descendants forever" (Genesis 13:14,15). Abraham lived as a stranger but with the Lord. His pilgrimage was represented in his life in the tent and his relationship with the Lord was represented in the altar which he built everywhere.

This stranger, satisfied with the Lord, saved Lot from captivity (Genesis 14). The king of Sodom and the king of Salem, Melchizedec, received him and blessed him. (Genesis 14:18)

Was this principle, "I desire none from the earth besides You," ever shaken in Abraham's heart? Yes, it happened that he desired to have a son. When he desired to have a son, he fell into many temptations. Hagar (Genesis 16), Katora (Genesis 25), and even after he had Isaac from Sarah, he was tested by God when He told him, "Abraham, take your only son whom you love, Isaac and offer him a sacrifice on the mountains which I tell you" (Genesis 22:2). Because Abraham applied this principle, "I desire none from the earth besides You," because he loved God with all his heart, he rose very early and took his son, the wood and the knife and tied him a sacrifice. Therefore, God blessed Abraham who loved him more than his only son, and all his genrations were blessed. Abraham's heart was focused on God more than on Isaac.

The Lord Jesus said, "He who loves father or mother more than Me is not worthy of Me. And he who loves son or daughter more than Me is not worthy of Me" (Matthew 10:37). Our Father Abraham applied this commandment many generations before Christ said it. God meant to him more than his family, country, and his only son. It is a virtue to love one's family, but it should not have priority over God's love in one's heart. Love of the family should be within the love of God, not competing with it. The spiritual person loves all people as part of his love to God, but he does not love anyone who competes with the love of God.

No one competes with God's love. Therefore, true love requires self-deprivation. The Bible says, "Do not love the world, or the things in the world. If anyone loves the world, the love of the Father is not in Him. The world is passing away and the lust of it" (1 John 2:15,17). "The love of the world is enmity to God" (James 4:4). "No one can serve two masters, either God or the world." "What communion has light with darkness?" (2 Corinthians 6:14). God is the true light. Everything outside God is darkness. Anything that contradicts God and His love is darkness. We who have been invited to be children of the Light, do not participate in the works of darkness.

Darkness differs in its degrees, the worst degree is sin. If the trifles and material things of this world drive us away from God, then they are considered darkness which should not enter our hearts. We want God alone to remain in our hearts. Besides Him, we desire nothing from the world. We fight every desire or thought that interferes with God's love. One of the songs says, "I have no opinion, nor desire nor thought besides following You."

God's children may own money, but money does not own them. "Those who use this world as not misusing it, for the form of this world is passing away" (1 Corinthians 7:31). Hence, love of the world cannot be put beside God's love.

Lot

Another example is Lot and his wife. Lot could not reach the degree of self deprivation in which he would love God with all his heart and whereby he would say, "There is none upon earth that I desire besides You." That is why he chose the fertile land and did not choose the land where he could live with God. What was the result? The result was that he was made a captive (Genesis 14), and lost all his possessions. Then Abraham rescued him but still he did not learn a lesson and the righteous suffered daily from bad company. Then he lost everything in the destruction of Sodom.

Here we see the repentance of Lot. When the two angels called him to escape to the mountains (Genesis 19), he did not say, "My possessions, my cattle, my family!" But he finally said, "There is none upon earth that I desire besides You." He left Sodom owning nothing. The Lord was sufficient for him.

But Lot's wife who did not apply this principle, "There is none upon earth that I desire besides You," looked back and changed into a pillar of salt. She became a lesson to anyone who has other desires besides God's love.

The Disciples

Another example is Jesus' disciples. Simon and Andrew left their nets and followed Him (Mark 1:18). John and James, the sons of Zebedee, left their father Zebedee in the boat and followed Him (Mark 1:20). Mathew left tax collecting and his job, and others forsook their families and wives. Every one of them was repeating that verse, "There is none upon earth that I desire besides You." Also, Saint Paul who forsook his high position and authority and endured sufferings for the sake of Christ said, "I have suffered the loss of all things and count them as rubbish that I may gain Christ" (Philippians 3:8). Hence, he, too, was attached to this verse, "There is none upon earth that I desire besides You."

All of these, after forsaking all things, did not regret it. Everyone's feelings were: How can I desire something from the world after this Great Light has shone in my heart and I became all for Him and He for me.

The Monks and the Merchant of Pearls

Two other examples are the monks and the merchant of pearls. The monks who led pious lives of complete self-deprivation, did not possess anything. Rather, they vowed to live a life of voluntary poverty, and they rose above the level of the home, children, and materialism. They wandered in the wilderness in need because of their great love to their King Jesus Christ and said, "There is none upon earth that I desire besides You."

Some of these were princes like Maximos and Domadios, and some had high positions which they forsook like Anba Arsanios. Some who were rich forsook their riches like St Anthony, others who were married forsook their wives like Anba Amoon and Anba Boulos the Simple. They all said, "There is none upon earth that I desire besides You."

This reminds us of the parable of the merchant which Christ said, "The kingdom of heaven is like a merchant seeking beautiful pearls, who when he had found one pearl of great price, went and sold all that he had and bought it" (Matthew 13:45,46). This great pearl of great price is life with God, His fellowship, and His enjoyment. The wise man sells everything to obtain that life and says to God, "There is none upon earth that I desire besides You."

How beautiful is the motto for the monks: "Keep away from everything to be united with the One." This means that the heart remains untangled from everything and from everyone to be united with God. God satisfies Him, fills all His being and becomes his source of happiness and joy. All of our fathers lived with their thoughts occupied with God only.

Mary and Martha

The example of Mary and Martha. Jesus Christ visited them in their house. Martha was busy cooking, thinking that she was doing something good for Him. Mary sat at His feet, meditating and listening to Him, expressing her emotions to Him, saying, "There is none upon earth that I desire besides You." Jesus Christ praised her by saying that she had chosen the good portion which will not be taken away from her. But He said to Martha, "You are careful and troubled about many things, but one thing is needed" (Luke 10:41). This saying of a spiritual writer: "You have spent your life serving the house of the Lord, when are you going to serve the Lord of the house?" applies to what Martha did. Even service should not occupy us to the extent that we do not have time for fellowship with the Lord.

Moses

The Prophet Moses: between the palace and the wilderness. Moses the prophet lived in a palace and was considered one of the princes, the son of Pharaoh. He was surrounded by riches and authority. However, all that did not enter his heart, for his heart loved the kingdom of God. Hence, he was determined to live for the Lord saying, "There is none upon earth that I desire besides You," "esteeming the reproach of Christ as greater riches than the treasures in Egypt, choosing rather to suffer affliction with the people of God than to enjoy the passing pleasures of sin" (Hebrews 11:25,26). Hence, he lived with God: as a shepherd in the wilderness and as a wanderer with his people in Sinai, forsaking the pleasures of life in Pharaoh's palace. Moses did not desire anything from the earth, therefore, he deserved to be the speaker with God and the faithful in all His house (Numbers 12:7). "I speak with him face to face, even plainly and not in dark sayings; and he sees the form of the Lord" (Numbers 12:8). This was his relationship with the Lord.

Because Moses did not desire anything upon earth, the Lord Himself talked to him for forty days on the mountain and he became the intercessor between God and His people. The Lord accepted his intercession for them and made him shine on the mount of Tabor in the transfiguration.

Solomon

Solomon: His mistakes and repentance. Solomon was a great king, to whom God had granted dignity, royal majesty, and wisdom more than all who preceded him in Jerusalem. In spite of his wisdom, he did not tell the Lord, "There is none upon earth that I desire besides You." On the contrary, he said, "I made my works great, I built myself houses, and planted myself vineyards. I made myself gardens and orchards, and I planted all kinds of fruit in them. I made myself waterpools from which to water the growing trees of the grove. I acquired male and female servants, and had servants born in my house. Yes, I had greater possessions born in my house. Yes, I had greater possessions of herds and flocks than all who were in Jerusalem before me. I also gathered for myself silver and gold and the special treasures of kings and of the provinces. I acquired male and female singers, the delights of the sons of men, and musical instruments of all kinds. So I became great and excelled more than all who were before me in Jerusalem. Also, my wisdom remained with me. Whatever my eyes desired I did not keep from them" (Ecclesiastes 2:4–10).

Solomon rejoiced in all his labor, whose source was not God, nor His love and fellowship. He sinned to the extent that his salvation became very questionable. What about his labor? All this labor became vain. His story reminds us of Lot in Sodom.

Lot had wasted the harvest of all those years in the fire of Sodom. He had been there seeking the fertile land, and it meant forsaking the altar of God and His fellowship, struggling for riches, living in a corrupt society with its stumbling blocks, and marriages to wicked people. All that was burnt by fire and Lot ended up with nothing, just as all the labor of Solomon ended, leading him to conclude that: "All was vanity and grasping for the wind. There was no profit under the sun" (Ecclesiastes 2:11). Certainly the relationship with God is the steadfast, permanent and beneficial one in this life and the life to come. "What does a man gain if he wins the whole world and loses himself?"

The Martyrs

Our Fathers the Martyrs. They loved God, not only more than all the pleasures of the earth, but more than life itself. They suffered death for His sake, trusting that this life has a continuation with Him in eternity. Hence, they forsook the world with all that is in it and did not desire anything from it, not even to live in it Whoever loves God and is satisfied with Him is ready to forsake anything and everything for Him.

The Lord recompenses manyfold those who forsake anything for Him The Lord says, "Everyone who has left houses or brothers or sisters or father or mother or wife or children or lands, for My name's sake, shall receive a hundred fold, and inherit everlasting life" (Matthew 19:29). This promise concerns the reward. However, those who forsake anything for God, forsake it not for the reward, but out of their love to God which rules their hearts. Their love to God made them pious, and they said to the Lord, "There is none upon earth that I desire besides You."

This last verse applies not only to love but also to help. With this verse, Jacob, the weak and scared, was able to meet his brother Esau the strong and violent who had four hundred men (Genesis 32:6). Jacob did not have an army like this, but he had only his wives, children and male and female servants, and he had his prayer, "Deliver me, I pray, from the hand of my brother, from the hand of Esau; for I fear him, lest he come and attack me and the mother with the children. For You said,'I will surely treat you well and make your descendants as the sand of the sea, which cannot be numbered for multitude" (Genesis 32:11,12). I depend on your power and there is none upon earth that I desire besides You.

The spiritual person sees that God is His Shepherd and Protector. If a problem arises, he delivers it to God, for God and not himself, is the One who solves his problems. He says, "Who am I? What is my strength and understanding to be able to solve all my problems? Lord, You know my problems more than I do, You know all the hidden and apparent matters, all the obvious, hidden and future problems. Through Your wisdom, O Lord, You can solve all my problems. Through Your love, You want to solve them for I completely trust that You love me more than I love myself and You care for me more than I care for myself. I am a child in front of You. 'The Lord preserves the simple' (Psalm 116:6). Therefore, I leave everything in Your hands, and have comfort in Your faith, trusting that You have many solutions, for 'Unless the Lord builds the house, they labor in vain who built it; unless the Lord guards the city, the watchman stays awake in vain' (Psalm 127:1). As long as You see my labor, this is sufficient, for You are the Almighty God who preserves justice on earth, and You are the Comforter of the weary who carries our griefs and sorrows. I do not worry about my problems at all, but I leave them in Your hands and there is none upon earth that I desire besides You."

Whoever meets God does not need any other power, for his power is God Himself. He says with David the Psalmist, "The Lord is my strength and song and He has become my salvation" (Psalm 118:14). His strength is not in the weapons of this world, nor in human help, but in God Himself.

"It is better to trust in the Lord than to put confidence in princes" (Psalm 118:8,9).

Also, David the Psalmist says, "God is our refuge and strength, a very present help in trouble. The Lord of hosts is with us; the God of Jacob is our refuge" (Psalm 46:1,7). This is the kind of person that sees that God Himself is his strength. He does not depend on himself, nor on his talents, intelligence, capabilities or human hand or human plans. God is sufficient for him, with Him he conquers, and God leads him to His victory.

He does not think how to talk when confronted by an enemy, for God speaks through him. "For it is not you who speak, but the Spirit of your Father who speaks in you" (Matthew 10:20). You do not defend yourselves, but "Stand still and see the salvation of the Lord" (Exodus 14:13,14). The Lord is your strength and salvation. Whoever is satisfied with the Lord does not need any other power, but says, "There is none upon earth that I desire besides You."

With this principle, young David went to fight Goliath the Giant. King Saul offered David weapons and clothed him with a coat of mail, but he forsook them and did not use them. He came to Goliath saying, "You come to me with a sword, with a spear, and with a javelin. But I come to you in the name of the Lord of hosts, the God of the armies of Israel, whom you have defiled" (1 Samuel 17:45). Yes Lord, I do not own any weapons like him, but I have your name and your power. There is none upon earth that I desire besides You. David fought with this Divine power which spared him all the weapons of war, "For the battle is the Lord's" (1 Samuel 17:47), and God is the Conqueror in battles.

Gideon

Gideon: to whom the Lord taught a lesson. He gathered thirty-two thousand men to fight the Midianites, but God saw that this was a huge number. If the people won, they might think their victory was due to their power and great number. So the Lord kept decreasing the number and purifying them till their number reached three hundred. Gideon fought with the three hundred and won. This was in order to make them know that power is from God. As long as God was with him, he did not need the power of the army to win, for there was nothing on earth that he desired besides the Lord.

With God there is no need for human wisdom Often wise people depend on their wisdom and understanding rather than on God who says, "Lean not on your own understanding" (Proverbs 3:5). Therefore, if you walk with God, do not seek your wisdom or understanding, "For God has chosen the weak things of the world to put to shame the things which are mighty, that no flesh should glory in His presence" (1 Corinthians 1:27,29).

David the prophet who said, "There is none on earth that I desire besides You," also said in the same psalm, "I was so foolish and ignorant; I was like a beast before You. Nevertheless, I am continually with You; You hold me by my right hand. You will guide me with Your counsel and afterward receive me to glory" (Psalm 73:22-24). My wisdom does not lead me, but You hold my hand, Your counsel guides me, and there is none on earth that I desire besides You.

St. Mark

Saint Mark in his missionary work: Saint Mark came to preach in Egypt with neither human help nor human facilities. There were no churches, no believers and no financial resources. On the contrary, there were obstacles from existing religions, from strong philosophers, and from the Roman authorities. Saint Mark who walked to Alexandria with a torn sandal, said in his missionary, "There is none upon earth that I desire besides You." With God's help, he accomplished his ministry, preached the Word of God, and converted many to become God's people.

The Disciples' Ministry

The Twelve Disciples in their ministry: God sent them without gold or silver or copper in their moneybelts or bags for their journey, or two tunics or sandals or staffs. (Matthew 10:9,10) Nevertheless, they did not need a thing, for they were able to say, "There is none upon earth that I desire besides You."

By the gate called Beautiful, Peter did not have anything to give to the lame man, but he said, "Silver and gold I do not have, but what I do have I give you: In the name of Jesus Christ of Nazareth, rise up and walk" (Acts 3:6). Hence, the name of the Lord was sufficient and there was none on earth that he desired besides God.

The ego or the self

The Lord is sufficient for you in your service. You do not need gold or silver or human wisdom, but the Lord gives you wisdom. You do not even need yourself. The Lord said, "Whoever desires to come after Me, let him deny himself" (Mark 8:34). He also said, "He who loses his life for My sake will find it" (Matthew 10:39).

Therefore, stand before God stripped of everything. His grace is sufficient for you. Tell Him in faith and confidence, "There is none upon earth that I desire besides You." "I was like a beast before You" (Psalm 73:22). However, it is enough that You are continually with me.

But is it true that you do not desire anything besides God? Other things which you desire besides God may endanger your life. What are they?

The Weak Points and the Substitutes

You want to be happy in life. There are reasons for happiness. Is God the reason for and source of your happiness? Are there other reasons which make you happy besides God?

These other sources which make you happy are your weak points. The devil who knows these sources tries to tempt you.

The heart which does not love the things in this world is a fort which the devil cannot penetrate. However, the devil is watching and looking for what you like and desire and what makes you happy, so that he may use these to tempt you. Sometimes he presents you with certain situations, if you respond to them, he will tempt you through these situations.

In Paradise, Adam and Eve were offered the chance to be like God knowing good and evil. They liked this idea, and this was the weak point which made them fall.

On the mountain, the devil tried to know what would make Christ happy. The Lord had spent some holy time on the mountain in spiritual fellowship with the Father. The devil wanted to know if there were other things beside the Father which would make Christ happy. Hence, he tempted Him with food: Why don't you change the stone into bread, so you may eat and feed the people? Then, you will become popular and accomplish your message as a social reformer. However, Jesus refused the idea because He had a spiritual way by which He wanted to feed the people: with every word that proceeds from the mouth of God. He wanted to satisfy their spirits which could not live with this bread. Hence, the first temptation failed.

Then the devil tempted him with spirtual scenes, such as throwing Himself from the mountain top and the angels will carry Him. Upon seeing this, the people will believe in Him! Then he tempted him with the kingdom, so He may have authority over this kingdom and spread goodness through the earthly laws. However, these two temptaions failed because Jesus rejected them since He had come to save the lost through the cross.

The devil could not find any desire in this pure holy heart. He could not find any weak point. As the Lord said, "The ruler of this world is coming and he has nothing in Me" (John 14:30). This is the pious heart which is not attracted to the kingdom of this world and its glory, nor to the admiring looks of people nor to the changing of the stone into bread, nor any goal other than the kingdom of Heaven.

The trick of the devil is to find anything which makes one happy besides God.

However, the pious person, the bars of whose gates the Lord has strengthened and in whose borders made peace, does not need anything that the world offers, but is satisfied with God.

Is there any desire in your heart, by which the devil can tempt you?

The devil is ready to offer desires, even to the ascetic.

The devil never loses hope in tempting even the monks who have forsaken the world, died to the world, chosen voluntary poverty and over whom the prayers for the deceased have been read. But he offers them other desires besides God, and which the heart clings to!

Satan wants each person to stop being satisfied with God.

Once desires penetrate the heart and rule it, then the individual's happiness starts to be shaken. He, then, loses his peace, and his goal changes. After his gaol was God, he starts to have many other goals. He becomes lost in the world and deviates from God.

God becomes just a means to fufill his goals.

If he wants God, he wants Him not for Himself but to fulfill the goals which he desires. If he prays, he does not pray out of love and eagerness, but to request the satisfaction of those desires. God does not become the center of love in his heart but just a means!

Following are some examples of people whom the devil had tricked with certain desires. These became their weak points which caused them to fall. Let us start with the wicked:

1. **Ahab the king and the desire to possess:** The devil offered to Ahab the king the idea to take the vineyard of Naboth to add to his possessions. Ahab liked the idea. Hence, it dominated his heart and thoughts, and caused him to lose his happiness and peace. He could not rest until he possessed the field. Naboth refused, and then Isabel interfered. Naboth was killed and Ahab inherited his possessions. God's wrath was upon him, and Ahab perished. He had a desire in his heart, a weak point through which the devil penetrated. However, the heart which is above the level of these desires, whose portion is the Lord, cannot be tricked by the devil.

2. **This was the problem of Judas Iscariot.** He was one of the twelve disciples. He lived with the Lord, saw His miracles, and listened to His teachings; however, the Lord was not everything to him. Judas had other desires besides God. He loved the money in the offering box; the Lord was not everything to him as He was to the other eleven disciples. Judas could not serve two masters, hence he sacrificed the Lord and perished.

3. **This was the problem of the Jews with Christ.** The Jews were waiting for the Messiah. However, they did not wait for Him for His love, but they wanted Him simply as a means to save them from imperialism and from the brutality of the Romans, and to establish for them an empire to restore David and Solomon's reign.

They had another desire besides God, and God was only sought in order to fulfill this desire. When Jesus entered Jerusalem on Palm Sunday and was proclaimed King, they did not do so out of love for Him, but rather out of their self-love and their love to the kingdom of David. The self, the kingdom, the government, and the salvation from the enemy were the basis, not Christ. Hence, when Christ declared that his kingdom was a spiritual one, not from this world, they departed from Him and conspired to kill Him in the same week!

Is God your goal or just a means?

The greatness of the saints emerged from their satisfaction with God. God was their goal and their only goal.

They concentrated all their emotions in God and had no desires or weaknesses that the devil could use to make them fall. Hence, it was easy for them to forsake everything for Him, willingly and joyfully. They did not have any other goals besides God or other than God!

Evil people have weak points deriving from desires which tempt them, as we mentioned in the examples of Ahab the king, Judas Iscariot and the Jews who crucified Jesus. But what about God's children?

The devil tempts them with substitutes that may appear holy. For example, service: A person may know God, walk in His ways, and may be eager to serve Him. The devil does not hinder him at all from service, but he tells him, "Serve and I shall be with you." The devil gets that person fully involved in service to the extent that he does not have time to pray. Service becomes everything in his eyes. He devotes all his time, effort and heart, to the extent that he does not have time to enjoy God. You may ask that person: where are your prayers? Your meditations? Your spiritual readings? Where are the holy hours in which you bow in front of God in love and awe, in which you open your heart to Him and give Him your love and enjoy His love?

This person may tell you, "I am busy preparing the lessons, visiting those I serve, busy with the club, parties, trips, pictures, prizes, financial and administrative matters, library, and visual aids. How can I find time for prayer? Even if I find time, my thoughts will wander in these things while I pray!"

It is good that one is concerned about service and works very diligently and faithfully. But it is not good that service becomes a substitute for God.

Service is a spiritual means by which one expresses his love to God and attracts others to God's love. By no means should service distract him from God. Service should not be transformed from a means to a goal in itelf. It is not good that the spiritual life of servants, or of those whom they serve, dry up during service due to their continuous work, allowing no time for prayer and meditation.

Martha was serving the Lord, but her service kept her away from sitting under the feet of Christ and listening to Him. The Lord told her, "Martha, you are troubled and worried about many things, but one thing is needed" (Luke 10:42,43). Also, the older son, who served his father many years, but in his busy service, did not have time to form a relationship of love with his father, talked to him in an inappropriate way (Luke 15:28-30).

No wonder that a person's mistakes increase during service! Not only does his great involvement in service prevent him from the direct relationship with God in prayer, meditation, and love, but due to "Holy zeal", he starts to combat everything which he does not like. Hence, he insults, fights, raises his voice, condemnns others, and accuses others without any love. He thinks that he is thus defending the truth! He may even compare his righteousness with the mistakes of others as the Pharisee did with the publican.

All that may happen in service and in the church. Then you may look for the relationship of the servant with God, but you cannot find it. He has lost his inner peace, his fellowship with the Lord and his love. While he was trying to remove the tares, he himself became one of the tares! Service became a goal instead of God and caused him to lose the purity of heart. The Bible says, "Blessed are the pure in heart for they shall see God" (Matthew 5:8).

True spiritual service leads to God and is not a substitute for God. Hence, if you find that your service has drawn you away from your prayers, meditations, retreat and fellowship with the Lord, or if service has affected the purity of your heart or caused you to lose your meekness and humility, then you should realize that you have deviated from the right path. Service has become a goal instead of God, so be very cautious and try to correct your path.

Sit with yourself as Arsanius did and examine yourself. Arsanius used to examine himself continuously to know how he was doing. Calm down and examine yourself: what is your relationship with God and what is your true goal? Examine all the spiritual means which you practice, whether they draw you closer to God or whether you practice them in a superficial routine way away from the love of God? Did some of these spiritual means become goals in themselves. Have you deviated from the right path?

What we said about service can be applied to prayer and meditation. You may stand to pray without the devil preventing you, but he watches to hinder you from benefiting. While you meditate on a beautiful prayer, he may tell you, "How beautiful is this meditation. No doubt many will benefit if they heard it from you." If you like his idea, then he has succeeded in letting you get concerned with people and not with God. The devil may even proceed further telling you, "How do you guarantee that you can keep this beautiful meditation in your memory till you finish praying? Take a piece of paper and write it so you do not forget it." Hence, the devil has lowered you from thinking about God to thinking about people, from prayer to service, and he thus hinders your prayers in a way which is acceptable to you! Then you leave your prayers to write your meditations! This may be repeated several times! Hence, your meditations do not express your feelings toward God and your deep emotions toward Him, but they become a means for others to share your meditations and God is relegated to the sidelines.

The devil has convinced you to give more importance to service than to prayer. He has convinced you to be concerned with people more than with God's love. He has destroyed the value of concentrating in prayer and praying with awe and made you sit and write. Hence, he has occupied you with things other than God! Little by little, he may completely change the value of prayer in your eyes.

He may even tempt you in a different way when you meditate. He may make these meditations a subject for pride and vain glory instead of serving others and making them benefit. You may say these meditaions in a spirit of bragging and not service. Then the devil has used prayer and meditation for your harm and to draw you away from God.

Satan may cause you to give more importance to work than prayer! He may let you get involved in any activity and he may call it "Service". This activity may even lack any spiritual benefit, or it may draw you away from prayer. He may even tell you that this activity is prayer! Your prayers may be at any time or in any position, whether when you are walking in the street or when you are sitting or when you are talking with people, without giving any time to concentrated prayer whereby you really feel that you are in the presence of God.

These are all temptations from the enemy, even in the spiritual means. Be alert and keep God in front of you all the time. Have the discrimination which understands the conspiracies of the enemy, so that you may keep God in your heart constantly. Let God be your goal and your priority.

Be cautious of the favorite sins which are covered with the clothes of righteousness and which may come in clothes of lambs, hiding their identities.

Gradual Progress

Let God be your goal and proceed toward Him step by step. Definitely, you cannot start your spiritual life being perfect, and you cannot start it by having God become everything to you. However, start by knowing and loving God, and grow in this knowledge and love. Give to God from your heart and grow in this giving. Open your heart so God may dwell in it and widen the place of His dwelling.

Train yourself to forsake continuously some of what you like for the sake of God, till the time comes when you can forsake everything for Him. For example, let us take fasting: Is it just forsaking some delicious food for God? No, it is a preparation for you to forsake for God'sake everything that you desire. It is a spiritual period in which you strengthen the spirit over the body to get closer to God day after day.

The less you love the worldly matters, the more you love God. The most important thing is that you do not stop at a certain step, but rather progress continuously.

Be like the seed which becomes a tree, then grows and grows. The Lord Jesus said, "The kingdom of God is as if a man should scatter seed on the ground, and should sleep by night and rise by day, and the seed should sprout and grow, he himself does not know how. For the earth yields crops by itself: first the blade, then the head, after that the full grain in the head" (Mark 4:26–28).

This is the nature of growth: the seed, the blade, the head, then the fruit. Any seed thrown in the earth does not stop from growing. If it becomes a tree, the tree continues to grow everyday, even every hour and every moment. Growth is its nature whether you notice it or you don't. Definitely, if you are away from it for a period of time, you will notice the growth distinctly, and the tree does not get weary of extending upwards and does not stop growing.

Be like this tree which grows upwards all the time, and stretches to the right and to the left. It grows from a seed under the earth to a plant above the earth.

Likewise, take a lesson from the tree which grows. Devote time to God and let this time grow gradually. Give God from your emotions and love. Struggle that this love grows day after day, and that this growth appears in your life and relationship with God.

However, be cautious; if you cannot grow, at least do not go backwards. Then the Lord will tell you, "I have this against you, that you have left your first love" (Revelations 2:4).

Truly, it is a tragedy if God's love stops growing, or cools down and regresses, and you seek one of the good old days when the spirit was inflamed and cannot find it. Then one will cry saying, "I wish I was in the earlier months in which God kept me, where He shone His light on my head. Oh, that I were in the months past, as in the days when God watched over me; when His lamp shone upon my head, and where by His light I walked through darkness" (Job 29:2, 3).

If you go backwards, when are you going to reach the goal which is far ahead?

You have known God, this is nice; but please grow in this knowledge. You may ask: what are the limits of that growth? Frankly, there are no limits.

You have reconciled with God by repentance, have formed a relationship with Him by purity, and have had fellowship with Him and loved Him. What comes next? The apostle says, "That Christ may dwell in your hearts through faith, that you being rooted and grounded in love, may be able to comprehend with all the saints what is the width and length and depth and height to know the love of Christ which passes knowledge; that you may be filled with all the fullness of God" (Ephesians 3:17-19).

"That you may be filled with all the fullness of God." What a marvelous expression! Thinking of that expression, I stand perplexed. Whenever I ponder its depth, I find it deeper than my understanding! Indeed, who is able to comprehend "The fullness of God?" Who can come closer to that fullness, or at least to the fullness of love which attaches man to God?

"Be filled with the Spirit" (Ephesians 5:18). You should not only have a relationship with the Spirit, or be in submission and obedience to the Spirit, or have the Spirit dwell in you, but you should also be filled with the Spirit. No part of you, neither your heart, nor your thought, nor your senses should be free from the Spirit. The Spirit fills every part of you! What a high degree!

Have you reached the fullness of the Spirit? Have you emptied yourself of everything, so that the Spirit fills everything in you and you may live by the Spirit, and by the Spirit you mortify the deeds of the flesh? (Romans 8:13).

Look at St. John in the Revelation saying, "I was in the Spirit on the Lord's day" (Revelation 1:10). Because he was in the Spirit, he saw the heavens opened, the throne of God, Jesus Christ and His face shining as the sun in its brightness. All this was because he was in the spirit. Then, what is the meaning of "Be filled with the Spirit"? How do we reach that level?

If you have not reached that level, at least do not stop, but rather proceed toward it. You have to realize that if you are walking toward a certain goal and you have reached half way through or three-fourths, still you have not reached your goal yet. You should continue your struggle toward your goal very faithfully. This saying of the Psalmist will comfort you, "Blessed are the undefiled in the way, who walk in the law of the Lord!" (Psalm 119:1)

You should progress continually on the way to your goal, moving step by step. You must come closer to it day by day, each day more than the previous day.

"Not that I have already attained, or am already perfected; but I press on, that I may lay hold of that for which Christ Jesus has also laid hold of me. Brethren, I do not count myself to have apprehended; but one thing I do, forgetting those things which are behind and reaching forward to those things which are ahead. I press toward the goal" (Philippians 3:12-14).

You must come closer to God day after day. In your spiriutal growth and in your relationship with God, let your knowledge of God, your love to

Him, your abiding in Him, your service and spreading His kingdom increase day by day. While you are getting closer to Him, beware of the hindrances which you may encounter on the road.

Beware of the distracting goals which hinder you from God. God is your only goal and you have no other goals besides Him. However, the enemy, who wants to hinder your progress, offers you other goals which may appear to be all right, but his purpose may be to hinder your concentration on God's love. So be careful.

Believe me that the angels of heaven "which are sent to minister for those who will inherit salvation" (Hebrews 1:14), become very surprised when they see us occupied with trifle matters, considering them our goals and hindering our journey toward God!

Any desire not pertaining to that of God is a trifle desire which cannot truly satisfy the heart. As St. Augustine said, "Our hearts will remain restless, till they find their rest in You."

On our way towards God, if instead of progressing, we have stopped at some side goals which occupied our time, effort, health, emotions, and attention, thus distracting us from the true goal, we shall hear what the Lord had said to His people who had wandered in the wilderness, "You have dwelt long enough at this mountain" (Deuteronomy 1:6).

Therefore, progress and reach forward to those things which are ahead. Do not allow any thing to hinder you on the way, and try to cast away any desire which causes you to be lukewarm in your spirituality or which replaces God's love. Keep God only in your heart and do not let any thing compete with Him.

May the Lord be with you, strengthen you, make you grow and lead your steps toward Him, Amen.

Milton Keynes UK
Ingram Content Group UK Ltd.
UKHW050627240624
444644UK00009B/151